SOCCER MOM: A HUMOROUS ADULT COLORING BOOK FOR RELAXATION & STRESS RELIEF
(HUMOROUS COLORING BOOKS FOR GROWN-UPS)

ISBN: 978-0-9987522-0-4

Printed in the United States of America

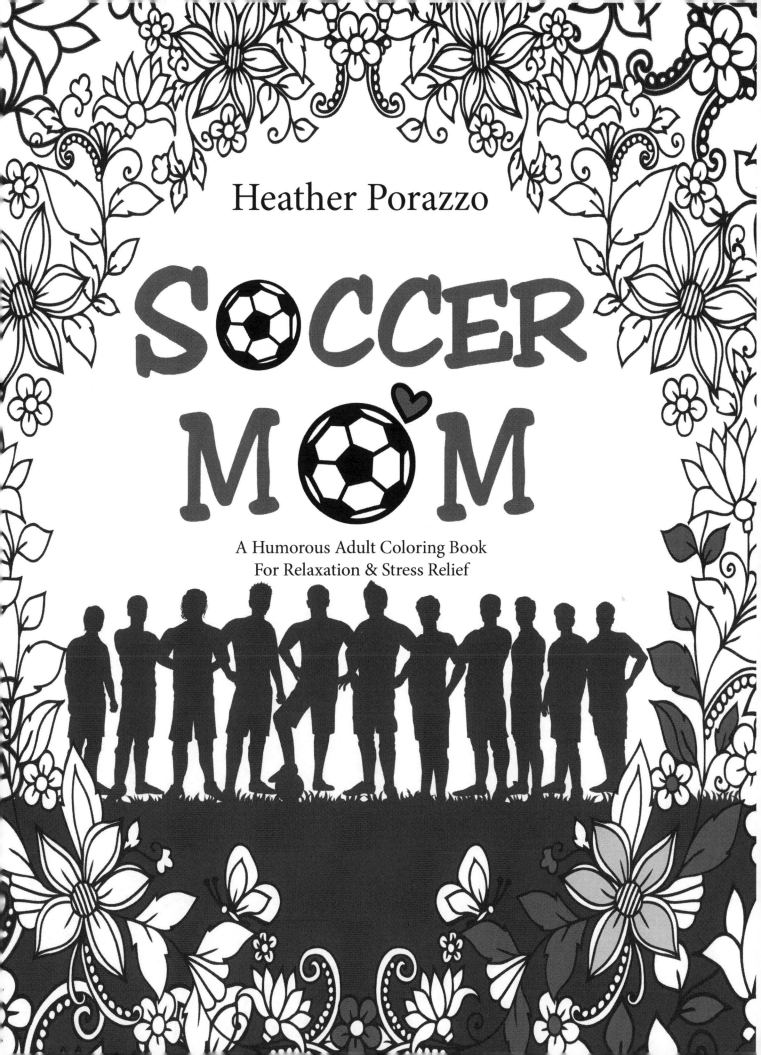

Dear Busy Soccer Mom,

Life's hectic, I know. But whether you're waiting in the car for practice to end, or you're at the gym or field, you deserve a chance to unwind, de-stress and let your creative side play, too!

So grab your favorite coloring tools and unleash your creative side, have a few laughs, and color in all the shades of "soccer mom life."

Sincerely,
Heather Porazzo

This book is dedicated to all of my fellow soccer moms, and in loving memory of my friend, Laura King.

Test Color Page

Shade	Color	Shade	Color

"Like a song, a mother's words play over again in her child's head and heart."

-Heather Porazzo

Words My Child Loves To Hear

Write your favorite inspirational sayings or
words of encouragement:

_____

_____

_____

_____

_____

_____

_____

_____

_____

_____

_____

_____

_____

_____

_____

_____

_____

_____

_____

Everyone's yelling about "offsides" and I'm over here in my happy place.

d

Shhh....

They're looking for a volunteer to be the
Team Manager.

e

Paparazzi Mom: she knows it's not the World Cup.
To her, it's more important than that: it's her child.

f

This year for Halloween I'm going as
my schedule.

GOALIE MOM

The most stressful position on the field.
Although the ball must get past every other player
before it can get to the goalie, the ultimate
pressure falls on her child.
Those moments can be stomach-churning
and she often finds herself holding her breath
until the play has passed...
Goalie Mom knows how hard her child tries
and how mentally tough this game can be,
but if there is anything she has learned,
it's that her child is tougher.

Away Game means...ROAD TRIP!!

j

Where the @#$%&! is field C5?

My work schedule fluctuates between
in-season and off-season hours.

k

ι

When someone asks you what day of the week it is, and you answer them, "Green shorts, white shirt day."

Mother's Day

Hey, Mom, why don't you sleep in late and take breakfast in bed? You deserve to be pampered!

Yeah, right. Your child's team is scheduled for an 8am "Mother's Day Tournament." Arrival time, 7:15am. Travel time to field, 30 minutes. It's 6:30am and you're already running late.

Breakfast and coffee to go!
Sigh. Maybe next year?

m

This Soccer Mom runs on coffee.

I'll think of the mud and grass stains later...
For now, the smiles on my children's faces as they
play in the rain is priceless.

My kids leave imprints of grass, mud, and clover sprinkled with turf, wherever they go.

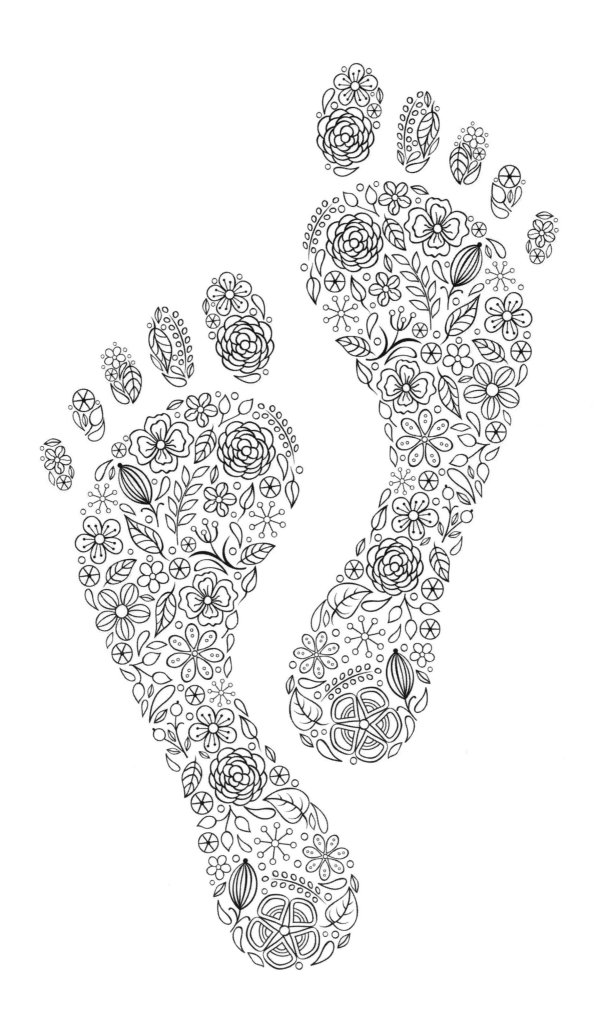

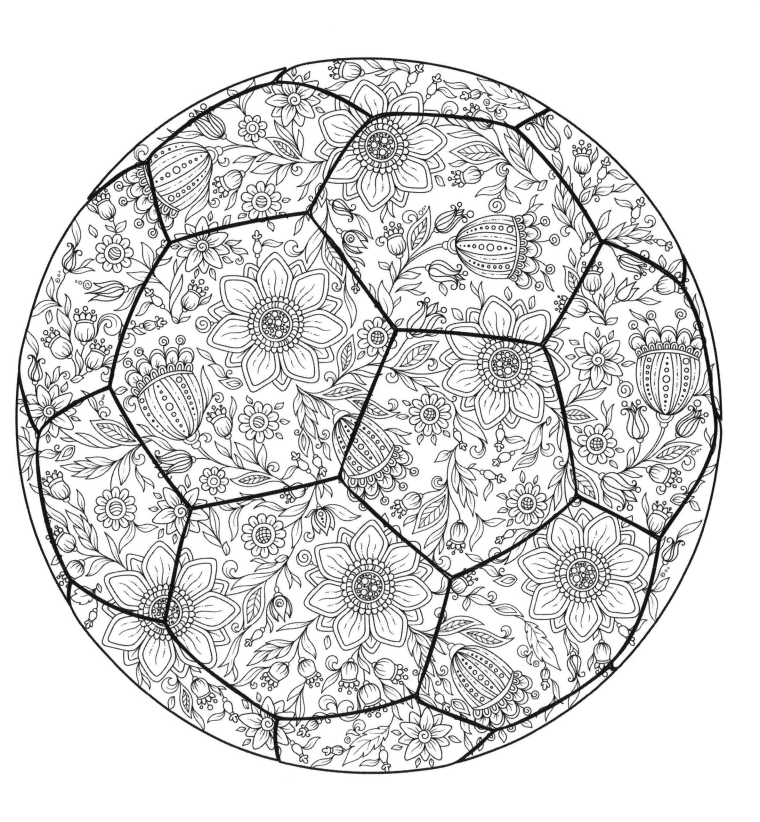

r

Every team has that parent...

"Man-on! That's okay, right idea- Unlucky!"

No Dogs Allowed?
My puppy isn't allowed on the field,
but some of these parents are?

t

u

Seriously?
Does anyone
really know
how to clean
Shin Guards?

Carpool
Music,
Mud and
Memories.

My carpool is packed like sardines. And after a weekend of games, my car smells like it, too.

x

I've hardly been home all weekend.
If I don't look at the mess when I get home, it won't really
be there, right?

Whether they win or lose,
ice cream is always the answer.

The Soccer Sisterhood:
Friendship formed through shared carpools
and between-the-games lunches.
These women cheer for your kids like their own,
and they always have your back.

z

aa

Every child has inherent talent.
Match a position to a player's strengths,
and they will shine.

Albert Einstein once said, "Everybody is a Genius.
But if you judge a fish by its ability to climb a tree,
it will live its whole life believing that it is stupid."

Soccer Mom Hair...the struggle is real.

It's an 8 am away game.
What did you expect my hair to look like?

Shhh...
I'm pretending to still be sleeping.

cc

dd

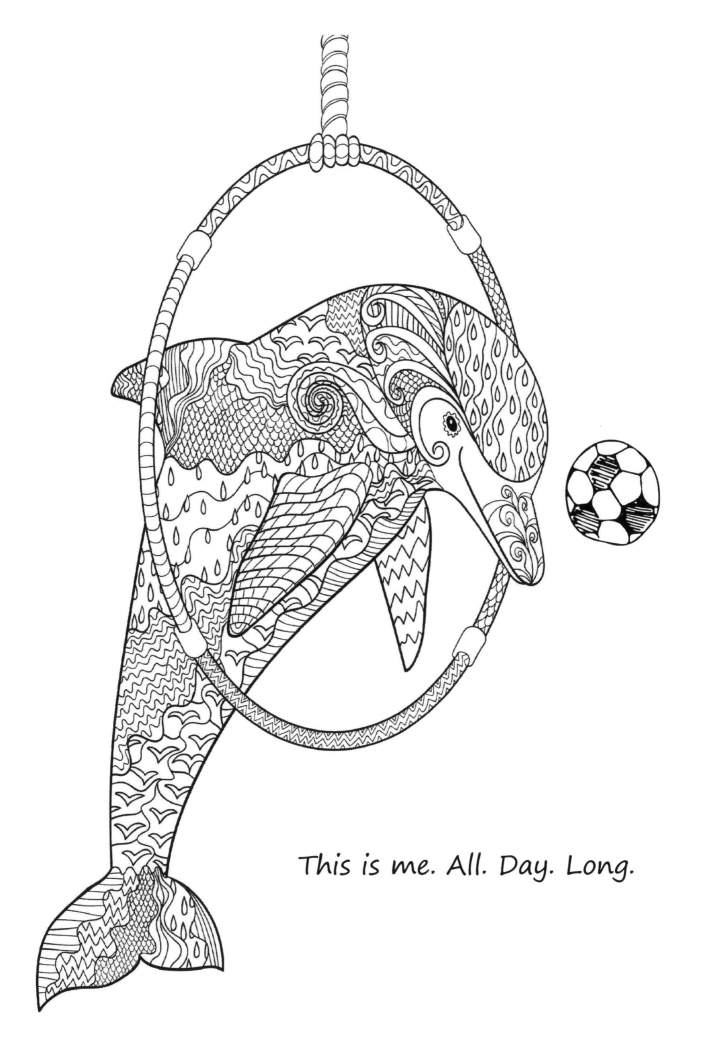

This is me. All. Day. Long.

Soccer Mom Life & Sailing

Soccer Mom Life is a lot like sailing. Despite the forecast, you never really know what the conditions of the day will be like until you're out there, in it. Maybe you were two hours away when the kid you brought to the game announced that he forgot his cleats at home. Or you dressed your child in green, and today's game was the white uniform. Or maybe you forgot to apply sunblock to your child before the game started...

Here's the thing, you're doing the best you can. You tell your kids to try their best because that's what matters, and you deserve just as much grace. So adjust your sails, and keep moving forward. Every boat takes on a little bit of water; it's part of sailing. And every mother has moments of mess-ups; it's part of motherhood. The greatest soccer players miss opportunities, and so do the greatest moms.

"Every boat takes on a little bit of water; it's part of sailing.
And every mother has moments of mess-ups; it's part of motherhood."
-Heather Porazzo

The look on your face when you see someone
kiss up to the coach
to try to get an advantage for their kid.

Never mind the sideline critics.
You're not playing their game;
you're playing yours.

Soccer Mom Shopping Trip

We still shop for shoes, but now the question is Indoor or Outdoor?

hh

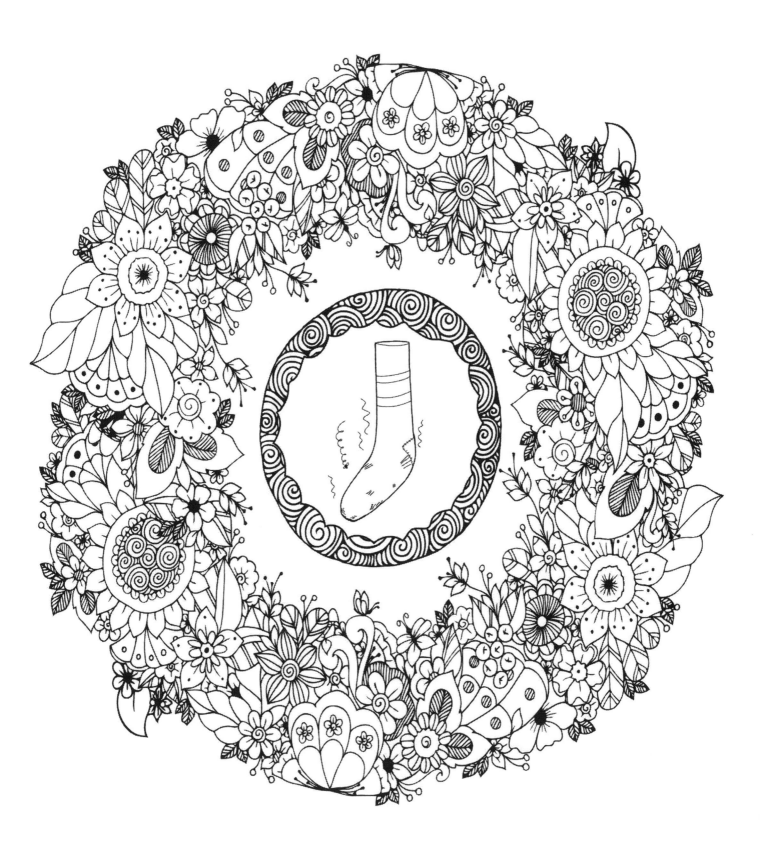

There are few things worse than finding a dirty soccer sock inside out, in a sweaty ball. If only they made floral scented athletic socks... Sigh.

This year's school science project will involve the half-full, sports drink my kid left in my trunk over the summer.

kk

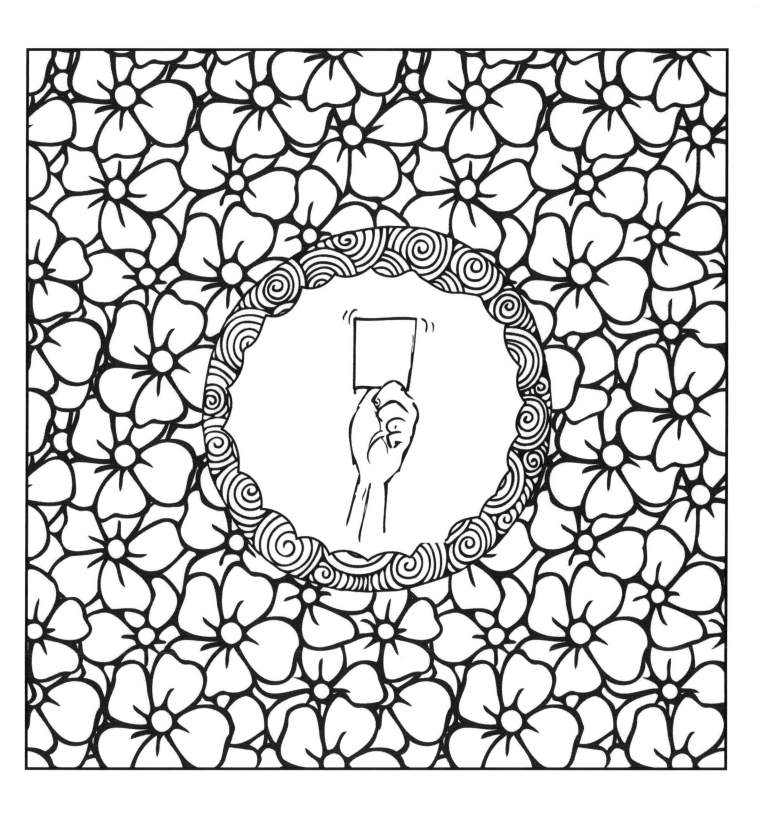

A Soccer Mom Card Trick
I keep a stash of ref cards on hand and flash
them as needed for warnings and time-outs.

u

Soccer Mom Savings Plan
My husband has put enough money in the
"Ref Criticism & Swear Word Jar" to fund a trip to
the Bahamas for two.

New Season
Schedule has been
posted!

I'm not gonna lie. I plan our family vacations around soccer tournaments.

Every Soccer Mom has a bit of Mama Bear in her.
She's supportive and nurturing, but if you mess with
her young, she'll tear you apart.

When someone asks me if I know why a play was called offsides.

Orange slices. Water. Protein bars...
If I ate like I fed my children, I'd be thin.

Side-line cuddles.
Sitting on a bench cuddling with one child
while watching their sibling play.

My children
don't always tell me
when they've out-
grown their cleats,
but when they do,
it's in the middle of
an away game.

vv

WORLD CUP

In our living room.
Every. Single. Day.

Every child deserves to have their own fan base.

Homework is often done in the car
on the way to the field or on the sideline
during a sibling's practice session.

Between the chaos, take a moment to look around at the beauty of the nature around you. Take a deep breath. Relax.

It was never about scoring the goal. It was about him believing in himself enough to take the shot.

Soccer Mom Book Worm

Why walk or gossip with other soccer moms during practice when I can layout and read?

Roses for you, Mom.
Because you deserve it.

THE MAN IN THE ARENA

by Theodore Roosevelt

It is not the critic who counts;
not the man who points out how the strong man stumbles,
or where the doer of deeds could have done them better.
The credit belongs to the man who is actually in the arena,
whose face is marred by dust and sweat and blood;
who strives valiantly;
who errs, who comes short again and again,
because there is no effort without error and shortcoming;
but who does actually strive to do the deeds;
who knows great enthusiasms, the great devotions;
who spends himself in a worthy cause;
who at the best knows in the end the triumph
of high achievement, and who at the worst if he fails,
at least fails while daring greatly,
so that his place shall never be with those cold and timid
souls who neither know victory nor defeat.

eee

fff

ACKNOWLEDGEMENTS

A special thank you to:

My husband, Patrick, for being my partner in this chaotic "soccer-parent life." Some of these pages were inspired by real events— some funny, some stressful, but all *worth it*.

My children, Jack and Luke, for their unwavering faith in me. I'm proud of the heart and character they both play with and live by.

Shelli Johnson, who listened to me brainstorm this book over a cup of coffee and who has walked with me every step of the way. I'm grateful for her guidance, editorial feedback and friendship.

Crystal Davidson, for sharing her goalie mom perspective with me during the editorial process and for giving this book her "soccer mom review."

Melissa Hyland, an amazing soccer mom and part of my "soccer sisterhood" who contributed ideas and the phrase, "Unlucky."

My mother, Barbara Laubinger, who managed to get her four children to their numerous sporting events over the years and who continues to devote herself to her family. I love you, Mom.

Laura King, I never realized how heroic being a "soccer mom" could be until I witnessed all you did to ensure that your child could continue to experience the joy of playing soccer—while you fiercely fought your own battle. With love, I dedicate my book to you, the bravest soccer mom I know.

Artwork and Image Credits

a. Image Copyright: <a href='http://www.123rf.com/profile_tanvetka'>tanvetka / 123RF Stock Photo</a>

b. Image Copyright: <a href='http://www.123rf.com/profile_tanvetka'>tanvetka / 123RF Stock Photo</a>

c. Image Copyright: <a href='http://www.123rf.com/profile_tanvetka'>tanvetka / 123RF Stock Photo</a>

d. Image Copyright: <a href='http://www.123rf.com/profile_tanvetka'>tanvetka / 123RF Stock Photo</a>

e. Image Copyright: <a href='http://www.123rf.com/profile_bimdeedee'>bimdeedee / 123RF Stock Photo</a>

f. 1. Heel and ball Image Copyright: <a href='http://www.123rf.com/profile_francovolpato'>francovolpato / 123RF Stock Photo</a>

f. 2. Border Image Copyright: <a href='http://www.123rf.com/profile_tanvetka'>tanvetka / 123RF Stock Photo</a>

g. Image Copyright: <a href='http://www.123rf.com/profile_annykos'>annykos / 123RF Stock Photo</a>

h. 1. Heart Image Copyright: <a href='http://www.123rf.com/profile_bimdeedee'>bimdeedee / 123RF Stock Photo</a>

h. 2. Goalie Image Copyright: <a href='http://www.123rf.com/profile_bimdeedee'>bimdeedee / 123RF Stock Photo</a>

i. Image Copyright: <a href='http://www.123rf.com/profile_yazzik'>yazzik / 123RF Stock Photo</a>

j. Image Copyright: <a href='http://www.123rf.com/profile_juliasnegireva'>juliasnegireva / 123RF Stock Photo</a>

k.1. Rose image Copyright: <a href='http://www.123rf.com/profile_tanvetka'>tanvetka / 123RF Stock Photo</a>

k 2. Working Woman Image Copyright: <a href='http://www.123rf.com/profile_moniqcca'>moniqcca / 123RF Stock Photo</a>

k.3. Ball from Image Copyright: <a href='http://www.123rf.com/profile_Lilia'>Lilia / 123RF Stock Photo</a>

l. Image Copyright: <a href='http://www.123rf.com/profile_helenlane'>helenlane / 123RF Stock Photo</a>

m. Image Copyright: <a href='http://www.123rf.com/profile_tanvetka'>tanvetka / 123RF Stock Photo</a>

n. Image Copyright: <a href='http://www.123rf.com/profile_bimdeedee'>bimdeedee / 123RF Stock Photo</a>

o. Copyright: <a href='http://www.123rf.com/profile_tanvetka'>tanvetka / 123RF Stock Photo</a>

p. Copyright: <a href='http://www.123rf.com/profile_kiyanochka'>kiyanochka / 123RF Stock Photo</a>

q.1. Flower Image Copyright: <a href='http://www.123rf.com/profile_karpenyuk'>karpenyuk / 123RF Stock Photo</a>

q.2. Ball shape Image Copyright: <a href='http://www.123rf.com/profile_francovolpato'>francovolpato / 123RF Stock Photo</a>

r. Image Copyright: <a href='http://www.123rf.com/profile_ljubovb'>ljubovb / 123RF Stock Photo</a>

s. Image Copyright: <a href='http://www.123rf.com/profile_olesiaagudova'>olesiaagudova / 123RF Stock Photo</a>

t.1. Background Image Copyright: <a href='http://www.123rf.com/profile_nuarevik'>nuarevik / 123RF Stock Photo</a>

t.2. Goal Image Copyright: <a href='http://www.123rf.com/profile_Lilia'>Lilia / 123RF Stock Photo</a>

u.1. Border Image Copyright: <a href='http://www.123rf.com/profile_tanvetka'>tanvetka / 123RF Stock Photo</a>

u.2. Woman Image Copyright: <a href='http://www.123rf.com/profile_greatnotions'>greatnotions / 123RF Stock Photo</a>

u.3. Shin guards Image Copyright: <a href='http://www.123rf.com/profile_greatnotions'>greatnotions / 123RF Stock Photo</a>

v. Image Copyright: <a href='http://www.123rf.com/profile_bimdeedee'>bimdeedee / 123RF Stock Photo</a>

w. Image Copyright: <a href='http://www.123rf.com/profile_kchung'>kchung / 123RF Stock Photo</a>

x. Image Copyright: <a href='http://www.123rf.com/profile_tanvetka'>tanvetka / 123RF Stock Photo</a>

y. Image Copyright: <a href='http://www.123rf.com/profile_bimdeedee'>bimdeedee / 123RF Stock Photo</a>

z. Image Copyright: <a href='http://www.123rf.com/profile_tanvetka'>tanvetka / 123RF Stock Photo</a>

aa.1. Leaf Image Copyright: <a href='http://www.123rf.com/profile_demonique'>demonique / 123RF Stock Photo</a>

aa.2. Children Image Copyright: <a href='http://www.123rf.com/profile_chromaco'>chromaco / 123RF Stock Photo</a>

bb. Image Copyright: <a href='http://www.123rf.com/profile_kudryashka'>kudryashka / 123RF Stock Photo</a>

cc. Image Copyright: <a href='http://www.123rf.com/profile_tanvetka'>tanvetka / 123RF Stock Photo</a>

dd.1. Dolphin Image Copyright: <a href='http://www.123rf.com/profile_lezhepyoka'>lezhepyoka / 123RF Stock Photo</a>

dd.2. Ball Image 59959324 Copyright: <a href='http://www.123rf.com/profile_yokunen'>yokunen / 123RF Stock Photo</a>

ee. Image Copyright: <a href='http://www.123rf.com/profile_nuclearlily'>nuclearlily / 123RF Stock Photo</a>

ff. Image Copyright: <a href='http://www.123rf.com/profile_helenlane'>helenlane / 123RF Stock Photo</a>

gg. Image Copyright: <a href='http://www.123rf.com/profile_bimdeedee'>bimdeedee / 123RF Stock Photo</a>

hh.1. Floral Image Copyright: <a href='http://www.123rf.com/profile_tanvetka'>tanvetka / 123RF Stock Photo</a>

hh.2. Shopping Image Copyright: <a href='http://www.123rf.com/profile_olillia'>olillia / 123RF Stock Photo</a>

ii.1. Sock Image Copyright: <a href='http://www.123rf.com/profile_theblackrhino'>theblackrhino / 123RF Stock Photo</a>

ii.2. Wreath Image Copyright: <a href='http://www.123rf.com/profile_tanvetka'>tanvetka / 123RF Stock Photo</a>

jj. Image Copyright: <a href='http://www.123rf.com/profile_tanvetka'>tanvetka / 123RF Stock Photo</a>

kk.1. Floral Image Copyright: <a href='http://www.123rf.com/profile_tanvetka'>tanvetka / 123RF Stock Photo</a>

kk.2. Card Image Copyright: <a href='http://www.123rf.com/profile_dicogm'>dicogm / 123RF Stock Photo</a>

ll.1 Wave Border Image Copyright: <a href='http://www.123rf.com/profile_helenlane'>helenlane / 123RF Stock Photo</a>

ll.2. Jar Image Copyright: <a href='http://www.123rf.com/profile_katjagerasimova'>katjagerasimova / 123RF Stock Photo</a>

mm. Computer Image Copyright: <a href='http://www.123rf.com/profile_bimdeedee'>bimdeedee /

nn. Image Copyright: <a href='http://www.123rf.com/profile_franzidraws'>franzidraws / 123RF Stock Photo</a>

oo.1. Ball Image Copyright: <a href='http://www.123rf.com/profile_concordcollections'>concordcollections / 123RF Stock Photo</a>

oo.2. Bear Image Copyright: <a href='http://www.123rf.com/profile_tanvetka'>tanvetka / 123RF Stock Photo</a>

pp.1 Border Image Copyright: <a href='http://www.123rf.com/profile_nuarevik'>nuarevik / 123RF Stock Photo</a>

pp.2. Woman Image Copyright: <a href='http://www.123rf.com/profile_franzidraws'>franzidraws / 123RF Stock Photo</a>

Artwork and Image Credits

Additional credits

Jack and Luke Porazzo after Jack's team won the Championship Game, 2016.

The cause for my joy— my children. They keep me busy! I admit it, our schedule is hectic and at times, exhausting. But when I see my boys on the field, doing their thing...it's all worth it. There's nothing like seeing my child develop confidence in himself, or the pride I feel when I witness them dig deep within to overcome adversity. I don't think I'll ever truly understand all the ins and outs of the offsides rule, but I do understand that my kids feel absolute joy while playing this game. And nothing brings me more happiness than seeing my kids happy. But I don't have to explain any of this to you. You get it, because you're a Soccer Mom, too.

Mud and Memories. Luke Porazzo after a game.

Photographer Shelli Johnson

Heather Porazzo is a clinical systems analyst, author, and the owner of La Perle Press. She lives in South Carolina with her husband, Patrick, and their two sons, Jack and Luke. When she's not writing she can often be found (and heard!) in the stands cheering on her favorite soccer players— her sons.

Watch For More Books By Heather:

Soccer Mom Season Planner Coloring Book

What Is Autism? The Story Of The Butterfly's Flight: How To Explain Autism Spectrum Disorder (ASD) To Children. An Interactive Autism Awareness Book For Kids!

Get A Free Soccer Mom Coloring Page Not Included In This Book!
Receive a free soccer mom coloring page PDF download when you subscribe to my newsletter at www.heatherporazzo.com.

www.laperlepress.com
www.heatherporazzo.com

Made in the USA
Columbia, SC
02 December 2020